MEETINGS

Anne Laws

Summertown
Publishing

Meetings

Published by
Summertown Publishing Ltd,
29 Grove Street
Summertown
Oxford
OX2 7JT

ISBN 1-90274115-3

First published 2000
Transferred to digital printing 2004.

Produced for Summertown Publishing by the
Linguarama Group Pedagogical Unit.

Printed and bound by Antony Rowe Ltd, Eastbourne

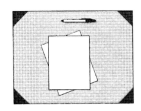

Contents

Preparing the Meeting

At the Meeting

After the Meeting

Use of symbols in this book

This warning symbol indicates **important points**.

This symbol is used to indicate a **hint** or **suggestion** to improve your meeting skills.

This symbol refers to other **chapters** with relevant information.

This symbol indicates **important cultural points**.

This symbol indicates that a **participant** is speaking.

This symbol indicates that the **chairperson** is speaking.

About this book

Meetings are held for a variety of reasons. To be effective, they should be constructive and useful. Effective meetings have to be worked at, they do not just happen.
All meetings need to:

- be planned carefully
- be run efficiently
- involve effective, well-prepared participants
- be followed up.

This book is designed to help you to run meetings and participate effectively in meetings in English. The book is divided into three parts.

- **Preparing the meeting**
  Reasons for the meeting
  Planning the meeting

- **At the meeting**
  Contributing effectively
  Chairing the meeting
  Participating in the meeting
  Intercultural meetings
  Formal meetings

- **After the meeting**
  Following up the meeting
  Reviewing and evaluating the meeting

Preparing the Meeting

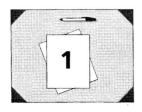

Reasons for the meeting

Participants need to understand why they are meeting before they can plan efficiently.

There must be a reason for people to meet. There must be something that they are hoping to achieve.

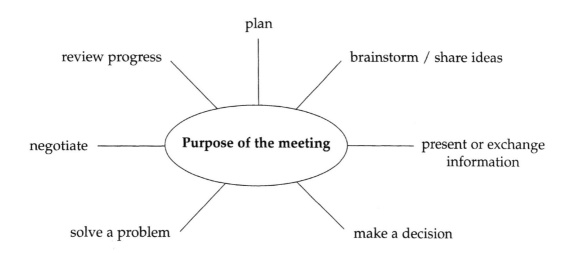

Planning

The purpose of the meeting might be to discuss a plan for the future and could include:

- agreement and approval of the plan
- discussion of the implementation of the plan.

There will often be a large number of planning meetings before final agreement. For example, most organisations prepare a formal annual plan for the following financial year: a **budget**. Other meetings may be held to plan projects and strategies.

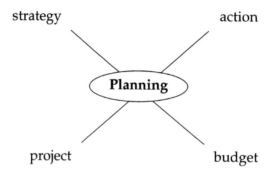

Brainstorming and sharing ideas

Meetings held for sharing ideas are sometimes called **brainstorming sessions**, where everyone puts forward his/her ideas. In these meetings, participants are encouraged to be as creative and wide-ranging as possible to collect the best and most comprehensive range of options as a basis for then shortlisting ideas for serious consideration.

Presenting or exchanging information

The purpose is to give information to other people. This might involve giving a presentation, followed by a question and answer session.

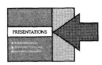 (See Business Skills Series: *Presentations*)

Making a decision

If the purpose of the meeting is to make a decision about something, there is usually:

- a statement of the decision reached
- agreement about who will take responsibility for various actions
- a list of action points at the end of the meeting, outlining what will be done.

Problem-solving

Meetings held to solve a problem usually begin with a statement of the problem. Participants then discuss their ideas for solutions, the advantages and disadvantages of each proposed solution, and try to reach agreement on the best solution to use.

Negotiating

Two or more parties meet to negotiate in order to reach agreement or make a deal.

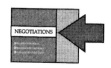 (See Business Skills Series: *Negotiations*)

Reviewing progress

In meetings to review progress, and to discuss and evaluate achievements, actual results are compared with **planned** results.

When actual results are unsatisfactory, the meeting will probably discuss action to improve the situation.

Planning the meeting

2

A meeting should be planned carefully. There are several matters to consider:

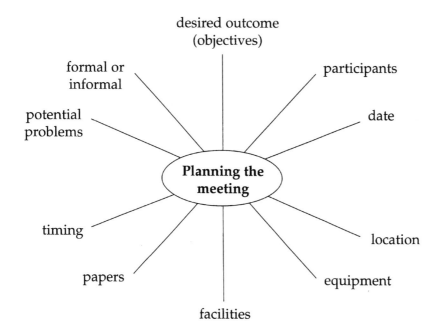

desired outcome
(objectives)

formal or
informal

participants

potential
problems

date

**Planning the
meeting**

timing

location

papers

equipment

facilities

Desired outcome

In order for a meeting to be effective, it is necessary to think beforehand of the objectives of the meeting. Individual participants should consider this when planning and it is advisable for everyone to establish this at the start of the meeting.

Participants

The organiser needs to consider who should be present at the meeting and advise everyone of the details.

Date

A meeting must be arranged at a suitable date. A meeting may fail to achieve its purpose if it is held too late, or after a lengthy delay. For example, a meeting to resolve a dispute should be held as soon as possible to prevent the dispute from getting worse. A meeting to agree to a plan must be held in time to put the plan into effect.

Location, equipment and facilities

The person who calls the meeting must decide where to hold the meeting and what equipment will be needed, for example:

- computers
- overhead projector
- flip chart
- beamer.

S/he must also check the facilities:

- Is there a room for refreshments?
- Who will provide refreshments?

Papers for a meeting

For some informal meetings and for all formal meetings, it is usual to have:

- an invitation
- an agenda.

Invitations

Here is an example of a formal letter of invitation to a meeting.

DEPARTMENT FOR REGIONAL TRADE
GOVERNMENT HOUSE

Mr D S Smith
ABC Industries Plc
Grand House
5 Oxford Road
London W1

4 September XXXX

Dear Mr Smith

The next meeting of the Committee for Business Affairs will be held at Government House on Friday 2 October at 10.00. The meeting is expected to finish by 16.00.

I should be grateful if you would let my Personal Assistant, Ms Baker, know whether you will be able to attend.

The agenda and papers for the meeting will be distributed two weeks before the meeting.

I look forward to seeing you on 2 October.

Yours sincerely

P. C. Evans

PC Evans
Chair, Committee for Business Affairs

This is an example of an informal memorandum to colleagues about a forthcoming meeting.

MEMORANDUM

FROM: James Campbell

TO: Alison Carruthers
           Alex Simpson
           Christopher Brown
           Nigel Dodd

DATE: 16 February XXXX

SUBJECT: Sales Meeting: 1 March XXXX

A sales meeting will be held at 10.00 on 1 March in the boardroom at Castle Hill. I will send you an agenda nearer the time. Please let me have any items that you wish to be included.

Agenda

The agenda is a list of matters for discussion. Here is an example.

PROJECT TEAM MEETING
TUESDAY 8 JUNE, XXXX, 09.00

AGENDA

1. Apologies for absence
2. Minutes of previous meeting held on 21 January XXXX
3. Matters arising
4. Software development
5. Computer installation
6. Training of staff
7. Testing of new system
8. Any other business
9. Points for action
10. Date of next meeting

Timing

You will need to consider the following questions:

- How much time do I have to prepare for the meeting?

- How long will the meeting take?

- Do we have a limited amount of time to make an important decision?

- Is this the only meeting on the subject or will there be subsequent meetings? If so, when?

Considering potential problems

It can be useful to predict any possible problems, for example:

- how to avoid wasting time and money. (A lot of meetings digress from the main purpose.)
- how to avoid the participants becoming argumentative
- how to discourage dominant characters from talking too much.

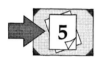 *Chairing the meeting*

If these things are likely to happen, consider what you could do to prevent them. Perhaps you could obtain the result you need without having a meeting or by having a limited amount of time and a very controlled agenda.

Formal or informal

The organiser needs to consider whether the meeting should be formal or informal. If a formal meeting is necessary, s/he will need to think about the procedure of the meeting and prepare the necessary documents.

 Formal meetings

Use this checklist before your meeting to help you prepare.

MEETINGS PREPARATION CHECKLIST

1.   What is the purpose of the meeting?

2.   What is the desired outcome of the meeting?

3.   Who should attend the meeting?

4.   What is the date of the meeting?

5.   Where is the meeting to be held?

MEETINGS PREPARATION CHECKLIST

6. What facilities and equipment are needed?

7. How long should the meeting take?

8. Is it a formal or an informal meeting?

9. What papers do I need to prepare? (invitations, agenda, minutes of previous meeting, working papers)

10. What problems could occur?

At the Meeting

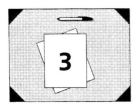

Introduction

3

When preparing for a meeting, it is essential to consider:

- how to contribute effectively

- your role at the meeting:
    - as the chairperson (sometimes called the **chair** or **chairman**)
    - as a participant

- intercultural aspects if it is an international meeting

- whether the meeting is formal or informal (formal meetings follow special procedures).

Contributing effectively

4

In order to make effective contributions to a meeting, participants need to be aware of some essential Dos and Don'ts.

DO	DON'T
• obey the ground rules	• monopolise the discussion
• be positive	• become emotional or too argumentative
• separate people from problems	• make personal criticisms
• keep to the topic being discussed	• digress
• use clear simple language	• use long complicated sentences
• allow others to finish	• interrupt too much
• ask for clarification if you don't understand	• pretend that you understand

It is important to make a good impression by contributing positively to meetings. How can you do this?

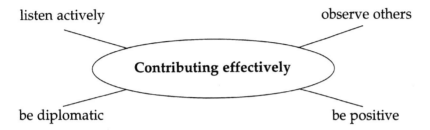

listen actively   observe others

Contributing effectively

be diplomatic   be positive

Listen actively

Listening plays a very important part in effective communication. Sometimes, people do not listen adequately to other participants and then cannot respond appropriately. They are more concerned with their own contributions than those of others.

Active listening is particularly important in international meetings where people are using a language which is not their mother tongue.

The following points contribute to active listening:

A ppear interested

C reate a positive atmosphere

T ell people when you don't understand them

I nterrupt only if absolutely necessary

V alue others' contributions by making positive remarks

E xamine ways to solve problems if you disagree

L ook at the person who is speaking

I ndicate that you are listening by your body language

S mile occasionally

T est your understanding later

E valuate as you are listening

N ote important points

I nquire with open questions later

N eutralise feelings by keeping calm

G ive feedback on what you hear

Observe others

When we participate in a meeting, we are influenced, not only by what we hear, but also by what we see. People respond not only with their words but also with their facial expressions, gestures, and body language. Observing what others do will give you some indication of how they feel about proposals at a meeting. The more you understand the other participants, the better you will be able to put your views over.

Observing is also vital when you are taking part in international meetings with people of a different cultural background. It may be useful to do research into body language, gesture, and the use or non-use of eye contact in cultures which are very different from your own.

W atch out for non-verbal responses

A ssess whether other people match their behaviour with their words

T ake notice of gestures

C heck degrees of formality

H ave awareness of your own body language and facial expressions

Be positive

Meetings are often held to solve problems. Conflict in meetings does not generally achieve anything. Therefore, participants should aim to be positive and should try to solve problems in a creative way. This has implications for behaviour and choice of language. The following points will help to contribute to a positive and potentially more creative atmosphere.

Spend time on small talk and relationship-building before the meeting starts.

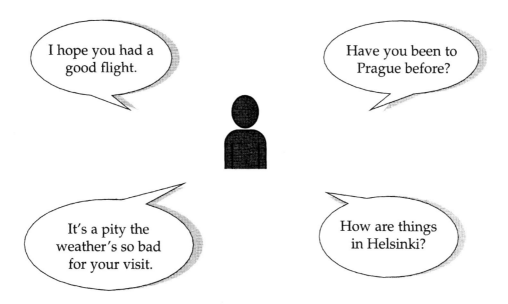

I hope you had a good flight.

Have you been to Prague before?

It's a pity the weather's so bad for your visit.

How are things in Helsinki?

Show respect for different behaviour and procedures in other cultures.

Signal your intentions. This is especially useful in international meetings as people will clearly understand what you are going to do.

Use positive language; don't be negative or sarcastic. If you disagree, make your disagreement positive.

Don't criticise others, but say how you feel. For example, don't say: "This is confusing", but say:

Try not to sound too forceful. When a speaker does not want to sound too forceful, **just** is often used as a softener in British English.

I'd   *just*   like to summarise what we've said so far.
Could I   *just*   ask a question?
I'd   *just*   like to clarify that.
Could we   *just*   go over that again?
Could you   *just*   explain that again?

Keep calm even when you are challenged. Be willing to understand the views of others. Ask other people to explain their objections.

Build bridges. If another person reacts negatively, you could make another suggestion:

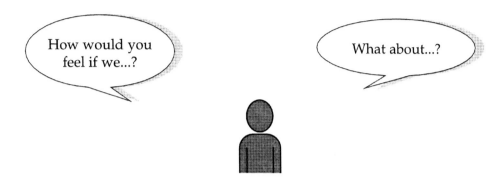

The listener has to 'cross the bridge' you have provided, and must answer you.

Be diplomatic

It is important, particularly in international meetings, to be diplomatic. English is much less direct than many other languages. The phrases on the left have been changed to more diplomatic phrases on the right.

BLUNT	DIPLOMATIC
We are not happy with this.	We would prefer a different solution.
That's wrong!	I'm not sure if that is quite right.
I can't agree to that!	I would find it quite difficult to agree to that.
You don't understand what I'm saying.	Let me explain that more clearly.

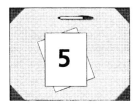

Chairing the meeting

The chairperson's duties

The role of the chairperson is vitally important because s/he runs the meeting. The chairperson:

- starts and finishes the meeting on time

- deals with all the official procedures in a formal meeting

- sets the ground rules

- ensures that the objectives are met

- controls the discussion

- encourages participation

- ensures that all views are reflected in the meeting

- summarises the decisions

- concludes the meeting and refers to future action.

manage and control the meeting

introduce the meeting

conclude the meeting

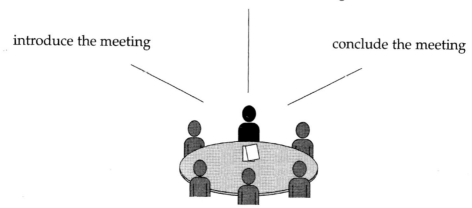

Introducing and starting the meeting

The start of the meeting is important because it establishes the atmosphere and sets the scene for an effective meeting.

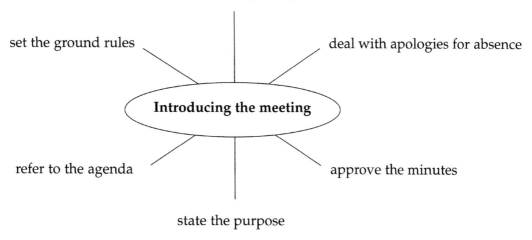

Here are some useful introductory phrases for welcoming participants and opening the meeting.

The chairperson reads out the names of absentees.

The chairperson asks the participants to approve the minutes of the previous meeting.

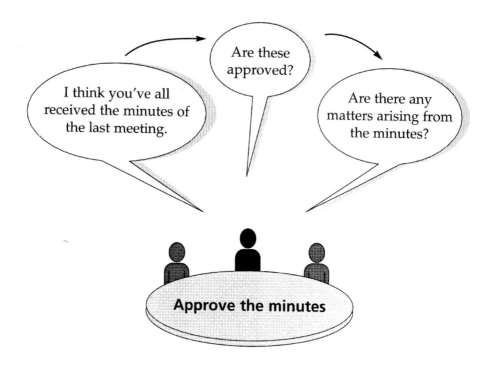

Here are some phrases the chairperson can use to state the purpose of the meeting.

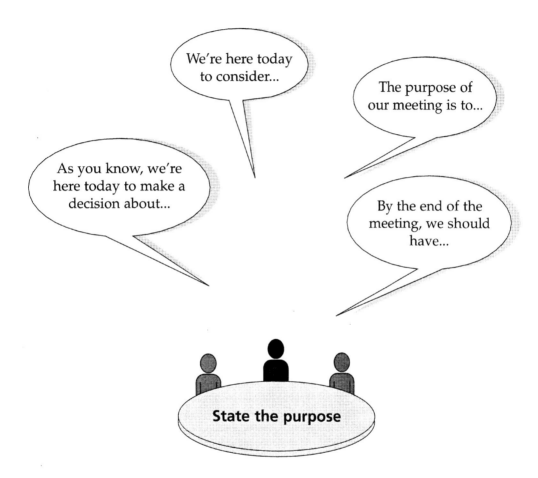

The agenda will normally have been sent out to participants in advance of the meeting. The chairperson normally checks that everyone has a copy of the agenda and then starts the meeting by referring to the first item.

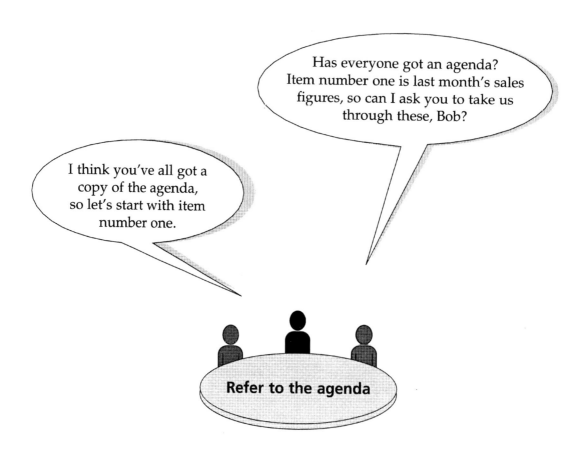

Setting the ground rules

In order to prevent problems from arising, it is sensible for the chairperson to set some ground rules at the beginning of the meeting, or when introducing a potentially problematic item on the agenda. Without rules, meetings can turn into long arguments. It is in everyone's interests to keep to the rules. Ground rules can help to stop participants:

- monopolising the discussion
- interrupting others
- becoming too argumentative
- disrupting the schedule.

A ground rule is a standard of behaviour expected from the whole group.

Here are some useful phrases for setting ground rules.

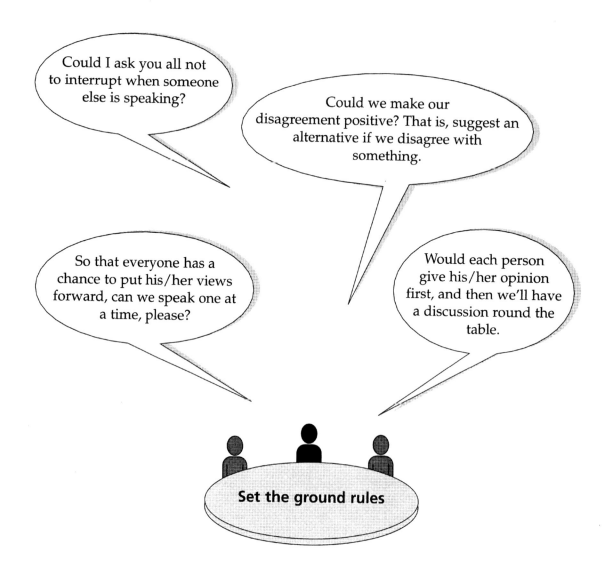

Could I ask you all not to interrupt when someone else is speaking?

Could we make our disagreement positive? That is, suggest an alternative if we disagree with something.

So that everyone has a chance to put his/her views forward, can we speak one at a time, please?

Would each person give his/her opinion first, and then we'll have a discussion round the table.

Set the ground rules

Managing the discussion and controlling the meeting

One of the most important duties of the chairperson is to manage the discussion and control the meeting. This means s/he should:

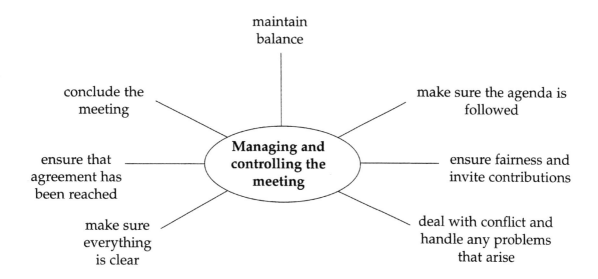

maintain balance

conclude the meeting

make sure the agenda is followed

ensure that agreement has been reached

Managing and controlling the meeting

ensure fairness and invite contributions

make sure everything is clear

deal with conflict and handle any problems that arise

These are important points in both formal and informal meetings.

For examples of language used only in formal meetings, please see Chapter Eight: *Formal meetings*

Maintaining balance

The chairperson should ensure that the meeting stays on track but should also allow sufficient discussion.

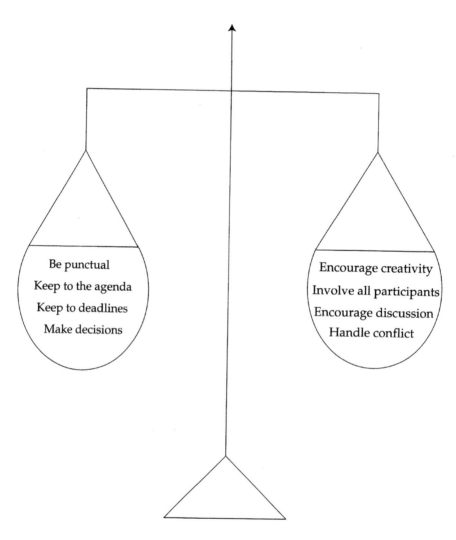

Be punctual
Keep to the agenda
Keep to deadlines
Make decisions

Encourage creativity
Involve all participants
Encourage discussion
Handle conflict

Making sure the agenda is followed

The chairperson ensures that the agenda is followed by:

- introducing topics
- indicating the end of a topic
- changing topic
- making sure participants keep to the point
- postponing topics
- returning to earlier topics
- ensuring that the meeting keeps to time.

The chairperson introduces topics.

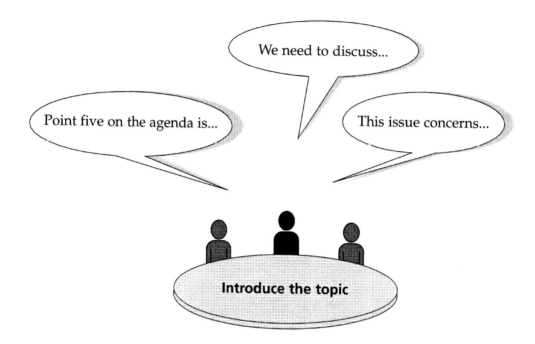

Indicating the end of a topic or a move to someone else

So is often used to indicate the end of a discussion topic or to give someone else a turn to speak.

> *So,* I'll summarise what we've said so far.
> *So,* I think we've covered everything on that point.
> *So,* can we move on to the next item, please?
> *So,* let's move on to John, now.

Right is often used in a similar way.

> *Right,* let's move on, shall we?
> *Right,* let me summarise.

The chairperson moves the discussion on by changing topics.

The chairperson must ensure that discussions do not stray from the topic.

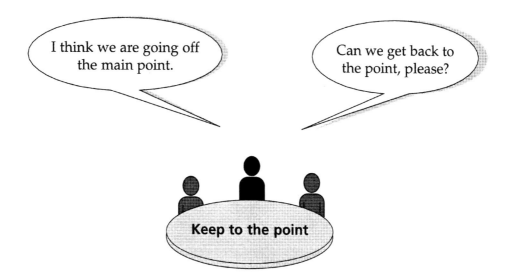

Sometimes, participants begin talking about a topic that comes later on the agenda. The chairperson may need to stop them doing this.

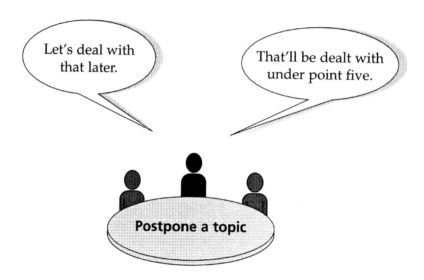

The chairperson may wish to return to a topic that was discussed earlier.

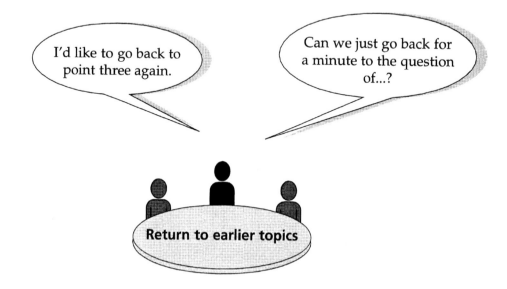

An important part of the chairperson's duty is to ensure that the meeting keeps to time.

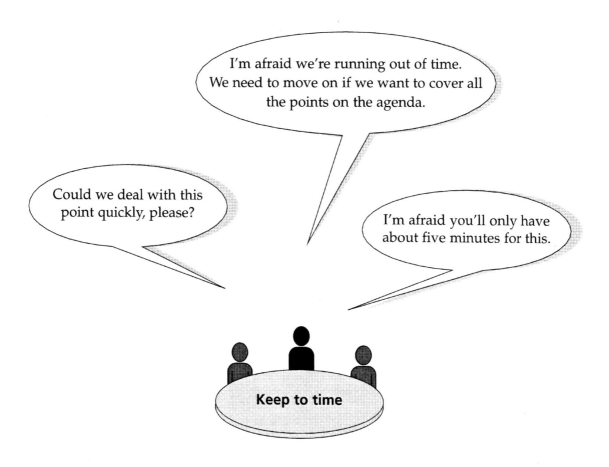

Ensuring fairness and inviting contributions

The chairperson can be compared to a football referee who has to ensure that all participants are treated fairly. S/he needs to listen and observe carefully. S/he must encourage reserved people to speak, control those who are dominant, and deal with interruptions.

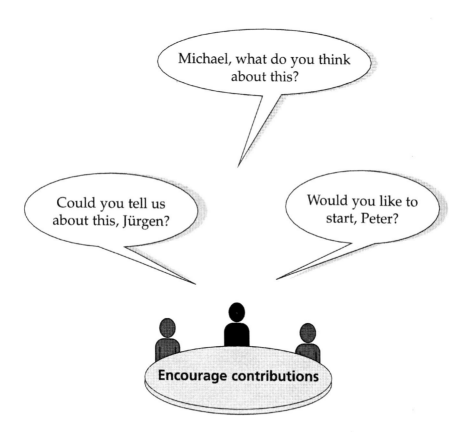

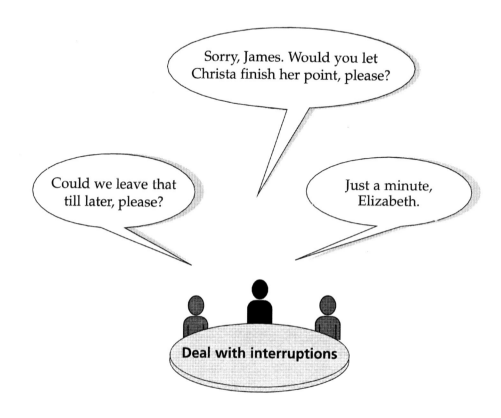

Dealing with conflict and handling problems

If people are becoming negative or aggressive, the chairperson must try to defuse the situation. It is useful to encourage participants to think positively. If they don't like something, the chairperson should encourage open discussion of their reasons for disliking it.

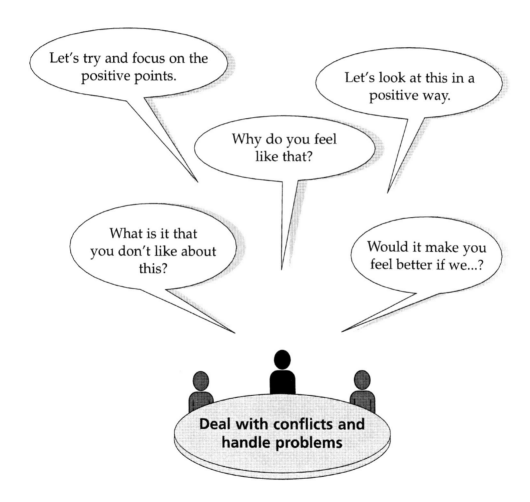

Making sure everything is clear

It is important to ensure that everything is clear and understood by all participants. The chairperson and other participants can:

- ask for clarification
- clarify points made
- restate and rephrase
- check understanding.

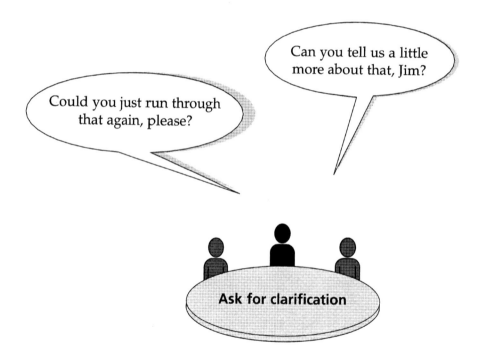

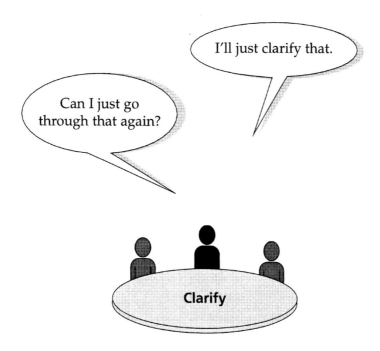

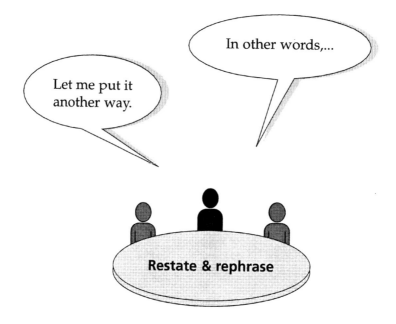

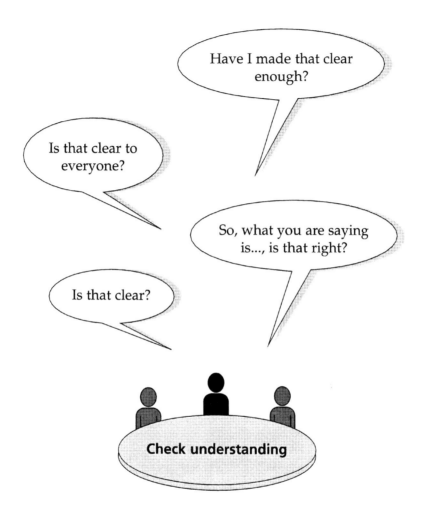

Ensuring that agreement has been reached

It is important to check that everyone agrees to a decision that has been made.

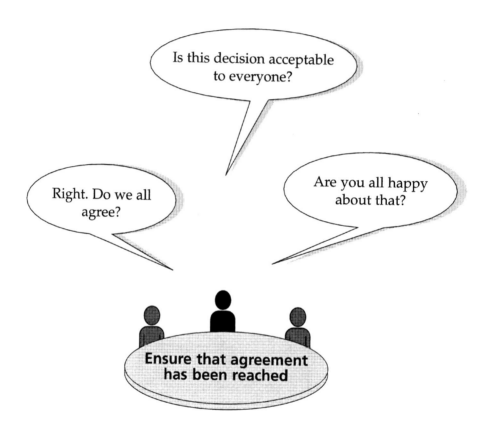

Concluding the meeting

In both formal and informal meetings, one of the chairperson's main duties is to ensure that results are achieved. These results need to be apparent to every participant. It is therefore very important that the chairperson summarises effectively and clearly. S/he should then refer to any necessary future action. The chairperson should then ask if there is any other business to discuss before setting the date of the next meeting and then concluding.

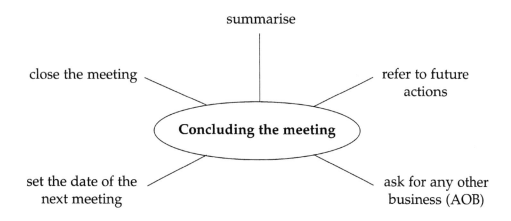

Summarising

Summarising ensures that everyone understands what has been agreed, that the results are clearly identifiable and they will be clearly noted in the minutes.

Here are some useful phrases for summarising.

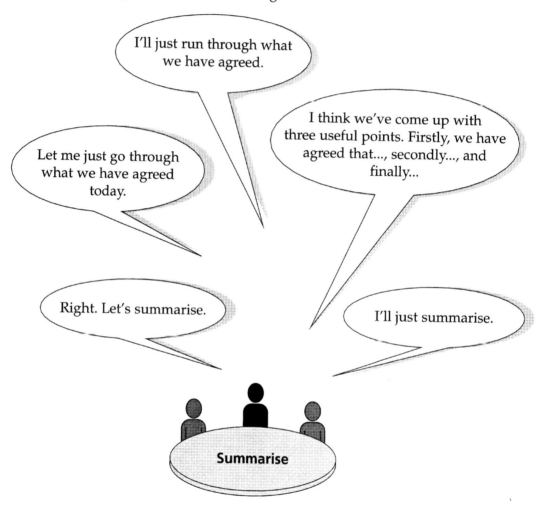

Referring to future action

The chairperson will need to check that everyone knows who is responsible for any future action and when the deadlines are.

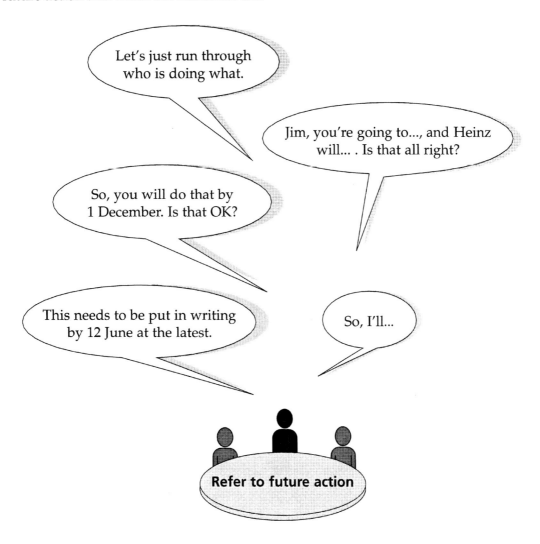

Asking for any other business

The letters **AOB** often appear at the end of agendas of both formal and informal meetings. They stand for **any other business**. This section of the meeting allows participants to raise any other matters unconnected with the main business of the meeting. After discussing and reaching agreement on the main items on the agenda and summarising, the chairperson usually asks other participants if there is any other business they wish to discuss before concluding the meeting.

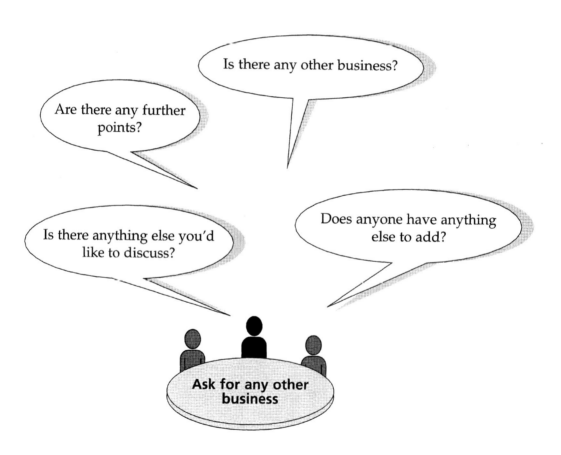

Setting the date of the next meeting

The chairperson may set the date of the next meeting before concluding.

Closing the meeting

Before the meeting finishes, the chairperson thanks the participants.

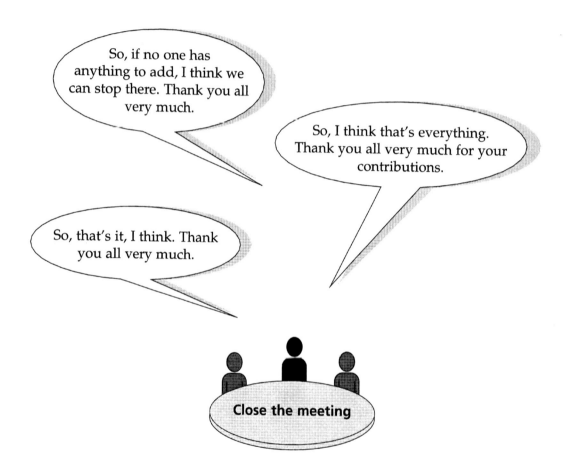

Use this checklist before your meeting to review and prepare useful language.

Will you need to do any of the following during the meeting? If so, write some useful expressions.

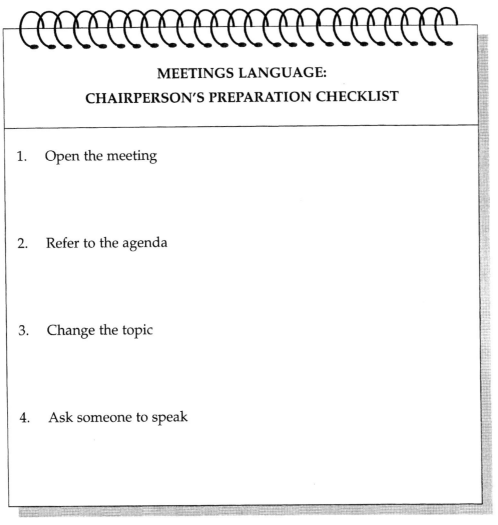

MEETINGS LANGUAGE:

CHAIRPERSON'S PREPARATION CHECKLIST

1. Open the meeting

2. Refer to the agenda

3. Change the topic

4. Ask someone to speak

MEETINGS LANGUAGE:
CHAIRPERSON'S PREPARATION CHECKLIST

5. Ensure that people keep to the point

6. Ask for clarification

7. Clarify something you have just said

8. Stop a participant from interrupting

MEETINGS LANGUAGE:
CHAIRPERSON'S PREPARATION CHECKLIST

9.   Summmarise the agreement

10. Refer to future action

11. Ask for any other business

12. Set the date of the next meeting

13. Conclude the meeting

Participating in the meeting

6

Before the meeting, you should decide on the kind of language you can use in order to get your opinions across effectively and to achieve the best possible results from the meeting. Try not to be argumentative or emotional and do not make personal remarks that may cause offence. Don't monopolise the conversation; let others speak. During the meeting, interrupt if necessary but think about when and how to do this. Try to contribute to a positive atmosphere by encouraging other participants.

In this part of the book, you will find some useful phrases to help you to be effective in:

- making your point
- communicating towards a successful outcome.

Making your point

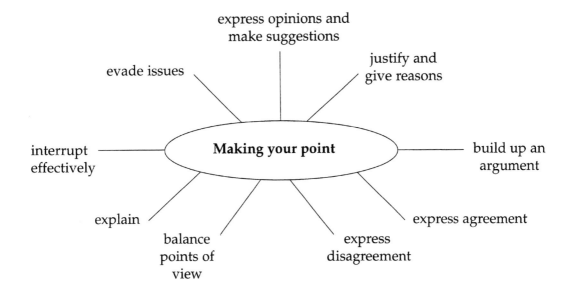

Expressing opinions and making suggestions

All participants should contribute as fully as possible by expressing opinions and making suggestions.

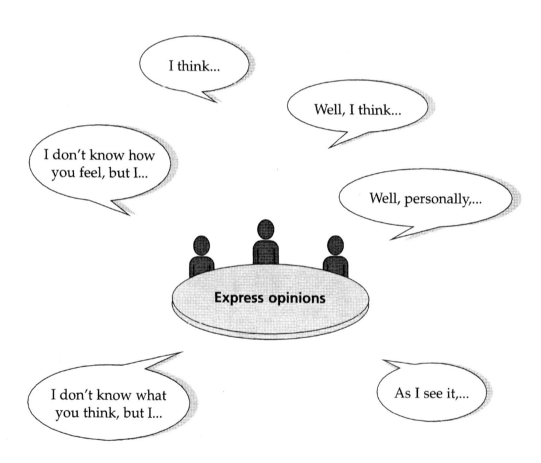

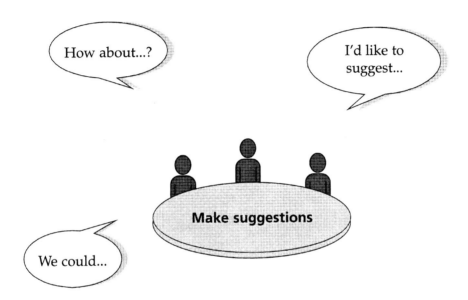

Justifying and giving reasons

Ensure you give a clear reason to support what you say.

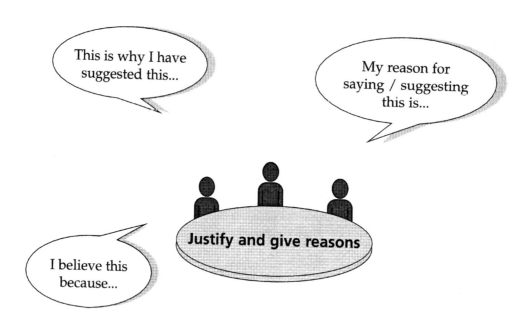

Building up an argument

You may wish to support your argument by giving more information. You may also wish to highlight advantages and disadvantages.

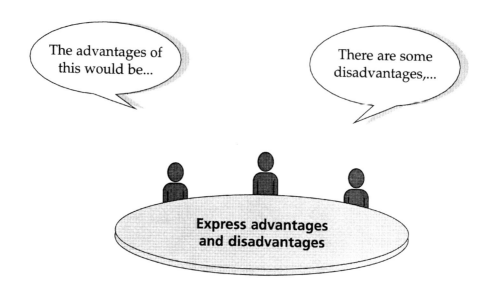

Expressing agreement

Expressing agreement about other people's opinions helps to move the discussion forward.

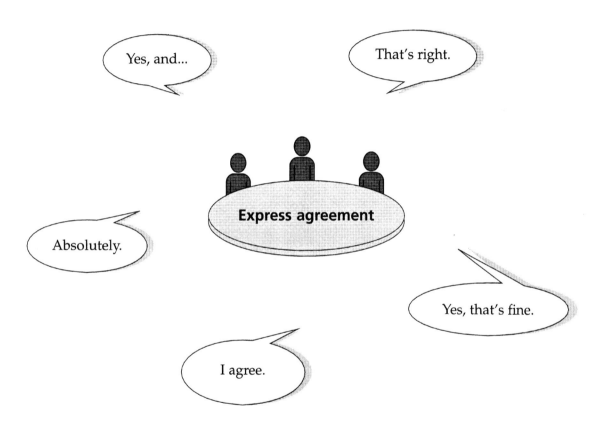

Expressing disagreement

Negative feelings should be expressed in a positive way as far as possible.

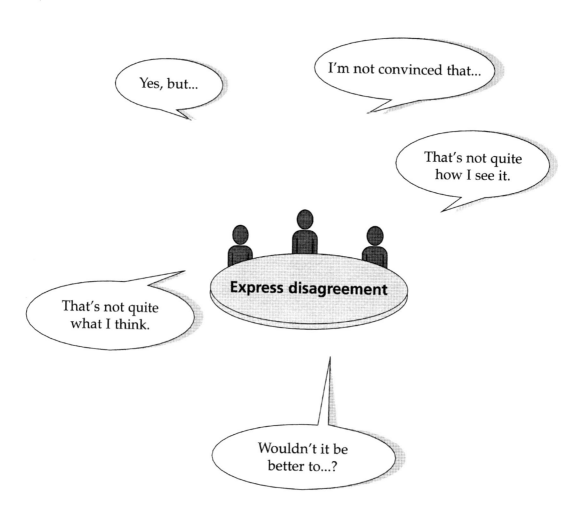

Balancing points of view

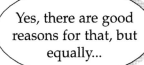

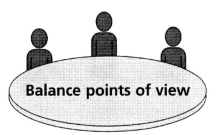

Explaining

If you think someone has misunderstood you, or you wish to explain something more fully, you can use these phrases.

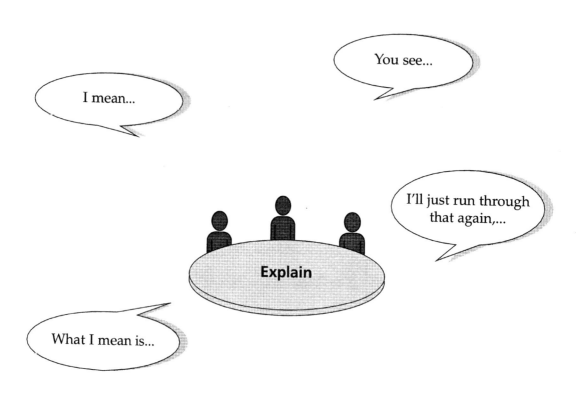

Interrupting effectively

You show respect for the other participants if you use one of these phrases before interrupting someone. This also gives a signal that you want to say something.

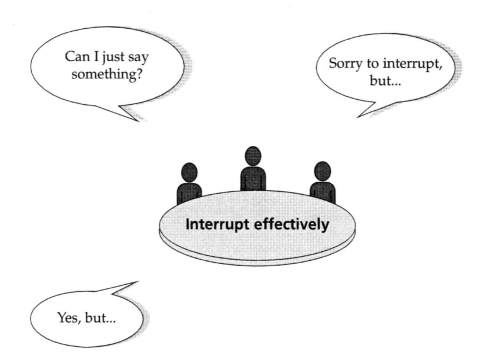

Evading issues

It can be useful to postpone discussion on certain subjects until later in the meeting.

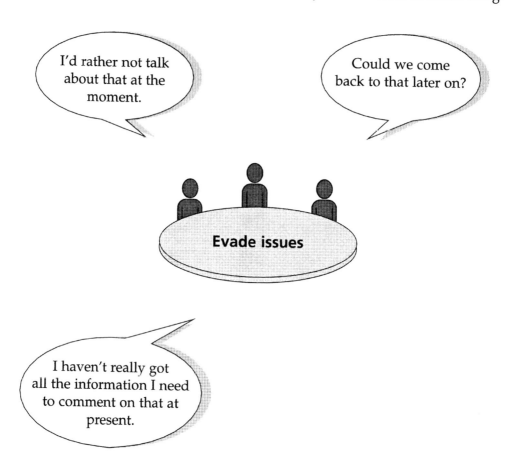

Communicating towards a successful outcome

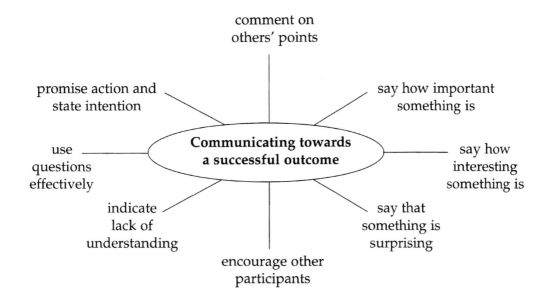

Commenting on others' points

When someone has expressed a point of view, make a comment on what has been said, if appropriate.

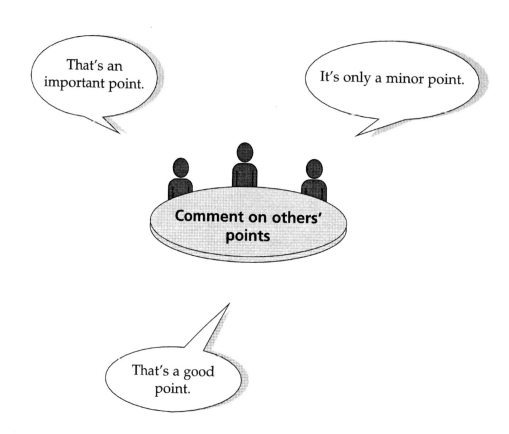

Saying how important something is

You can support others or back up your own arguments by emphasising the importance of a point made.

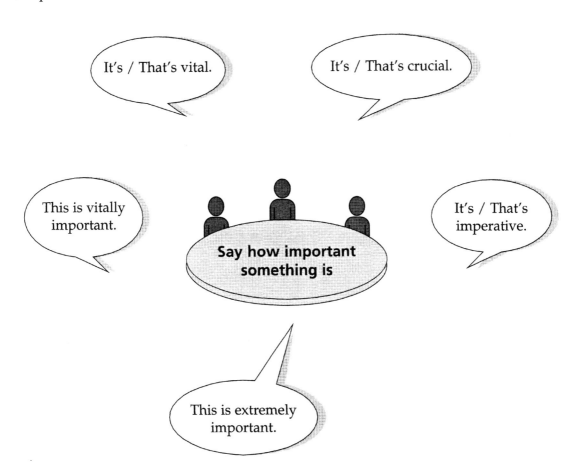

Saying how interesting something is

You can encourage others by showing interest.

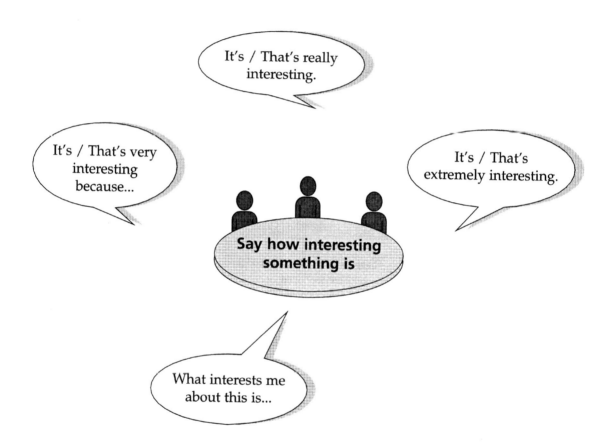

Saying that something is surprising

You may wish to express your surprise about something.

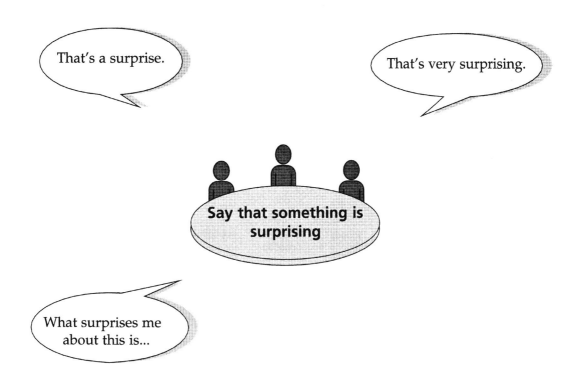

Encouraging other participants

If people remain silent and do not give opinions, ask them what they think. Silence can mean agreement or disagreement. You can help to move the meeting forward by encouraging others to speak and by giving others positive feedback.

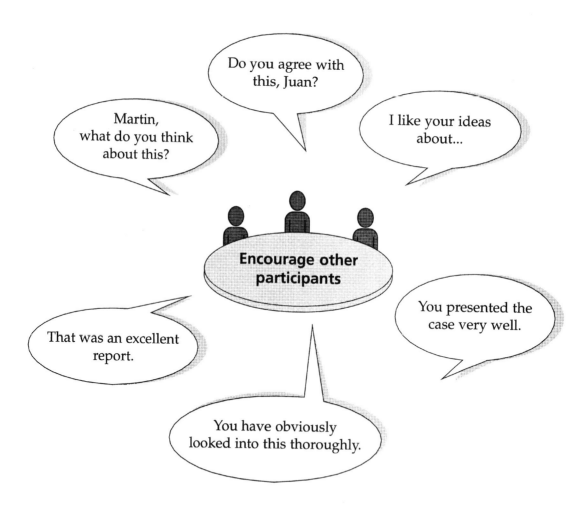

Indicating lack of understanding

If you do not understand what someone else has said, you can use these phrases.

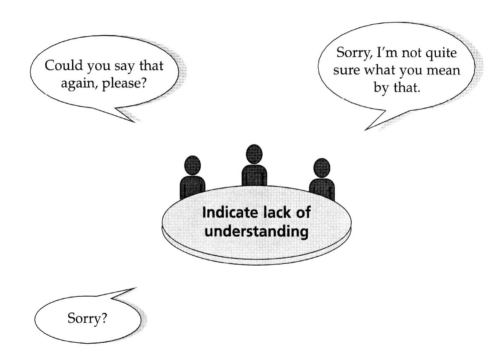

Using questions effectively

Questions can help to move the meeting forward and help to clarify your understanding of others' points of view. It is worth considering in advance the types of questions you might need to ask.

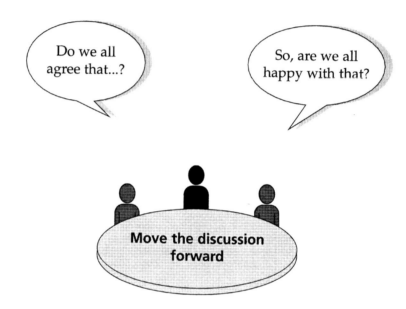

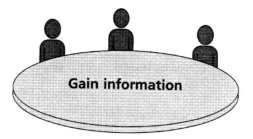

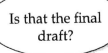

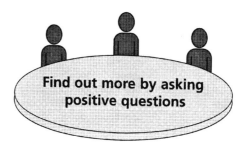

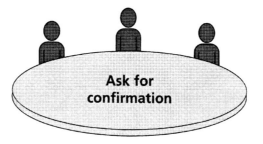

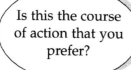

Promising action and stating intention

Say what you intend to do as a result of the meeting by using these phrases.

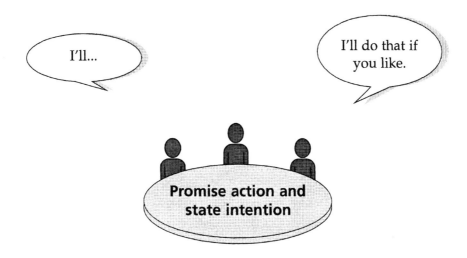

Intercultural meetings

Intercultural meetings can be less effective and more problematic than meetings between people of the same culture. However, they can also be more effective because people from different cultures often bring with them different skills and approaches.

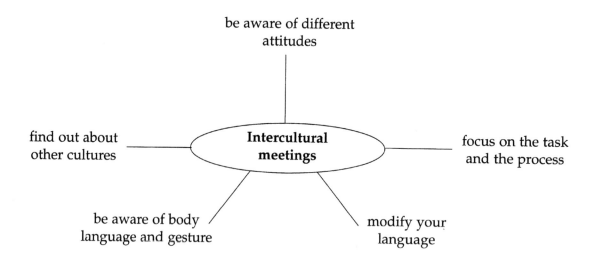

Be aware of different attitudes

People from different cultures may approach meetings in different ways. Some of the areas of potential difference are:

- amount of time spent creating rapport before getting down to business
- procedure of the meeting
- attitude to time (punctuality, deadlines)
- acceptance of interruptions during a meeting
- decision-making (who makes the decision and whether a decision is expected)
- attitude to risk and change
- attitude to women at meetings
- body language and gesture
- forms of address
- levels of formality in speech and clothes.

Use the cultural checklist on pages 110-113 to help you prepare, and do as much research as you can into other relevant cultures and their approach to meetings. When you do your research, concentrate on the areas listed on the previous page.

It is important in intercultural meetings that one culture does not impose its way of approaching meetings on others. The best strategy is to have open and honest discussion about the different approaches.

- Agree first of all on the desired outcome of the meeting.
- Then, discuss the different ways of reaching your objectives.
- Agree on the best way to achieve the objectives. The best way may not be your way or their way; it may be a combination of both ways, or it could be a third way.

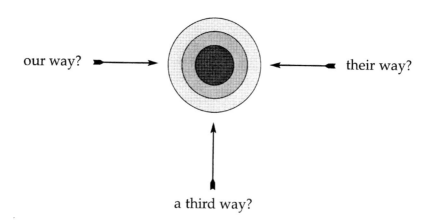

Focus on the task and the process

In all meetings, it is important to discuss the way in which you are going to do things but it is especially important in intercultural meetings where strategies and approaches may differ, where there may be differences in the use of English and when people may be suspicious of different approaches. You need to take special steps to ensure that:

- everyone knows and agrees on the objectives of the task
- everyone agrees on the process necessary to achieve these.

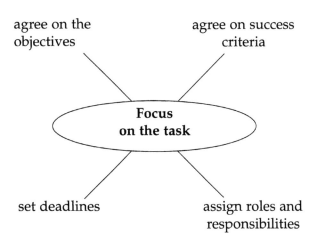

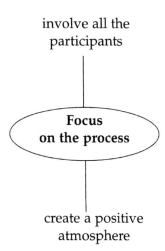

Focus on the task

Here are some useful phrases to discuss the task.

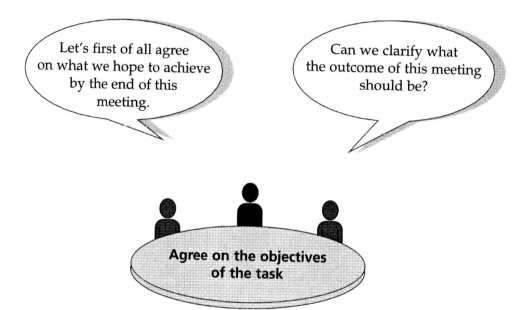

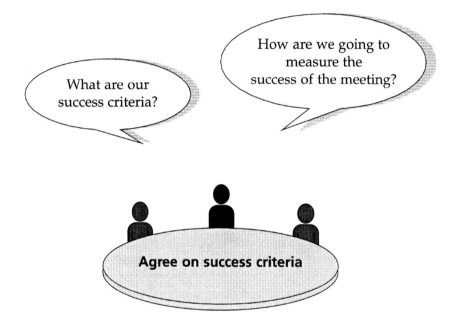

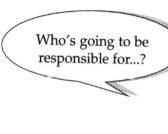

Focus on the process

Relationships are important and participants in intercultural meetings need to develop trust in each other. You may need to spend longer on making small talk and getting to know other people. Some people may not be as fluent in English as others. You need to ensure that everyone participates. If there are shy people in the group or people worried about their level of English, give them time to reflect before speaking, rather than by asking everyone to speak out immediately on a discussion point.

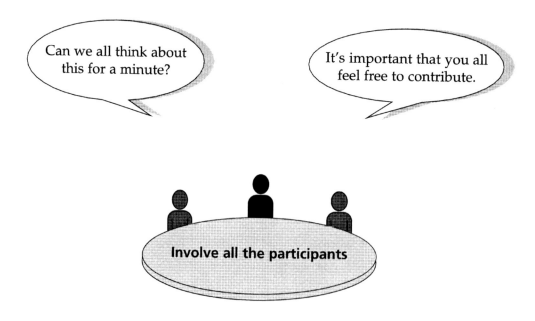

It is particularly important in intercultural meetings to maintain a positive atmosphere. This can be achieved by openly discussing differences and agreeing together on the procedures that are necessary. The following phrases are useful:

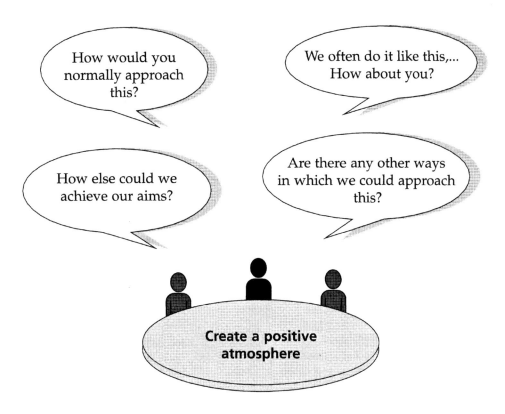

Modifying your language

In an intercultural meeting, it may be necessary to modify your use of English to ensure that everyone understands everything. You can do this by:

- using clear, simple language
- avoiding long complicated sentences
- speaking more slowly than usual
- avoiding the use of idioms and colloquial language
- clarifying what you have said
- checking your own and other people's understanding
- asking a lot of questions
- summarising what has been said.

You also need to allow people to have periods of silence to think if necessary. Silence is much more important in some cultures than in others. In some cultures, people leave a period of silence before answering a question in order to show respect to the questioner. It is also very important to show that you are actively listening when people speak.

 Contributing effectively

You may need to allow people to use their own language occasionally, providing that there is someone who can interpret efficiently.

Be aware of body language and gesture

Non-verbal communication can be very important in intercultural meetings. Try to modify your use of gesture. Find out if there is anything you should be aware of when meeting with people from other cultures. Eye contact, for example, may vary from one culture to another. In some cultures, maintenance of eye contact shows interest, in others, avoidance of eye contact shows respect. Handshaking and touching others may also vary. In some cultures, the way in which you present and receive business cards is very important. People from certain cultures may be unsure how to address you if they have not seen your title on your business card.

Find out about other cultures

There are a number of useful books outlining the results of research into other cultures and their attitudes to business meetings. You may like to attend a course about a specific culture with which you deal. Embassies are a good source of practical information. Talking to colleagues with experience is very helpful. It is important to remember that not everyone from one culture will behave or do things in the same way as everyone else. We are all influenced by our regional and personal backgrounds, age, education, and company culture as well as our national culture. The most important advice is to observe and listen carefully when you are in meetings and to discuss any differences openly and sensitively.

Use this list as a reminder of how to minimise language problems in intercultural meetings.

MINIMISING LANGUAGE PROBLEMS
IN INTERCULTURAL MEETINGS

1. Plan what you are going to say in advance. This will help you to choose clear and simple language.

2. Build rapport.

3. Use positive language. Don't be negative.

4. Build bridges. If someone reacts negatively, make another suggestion or ask why they don't like the idea.

5. Use short, simple sentences. Put one idea in each sentence. Other people's English may not be as good as yours.

6. Reduce your use of idioms as people may not understand them.

7. Signal what you are going to do. Say, for example, that you are going to ask a question, or make a proposal.

8. Ask questions to clarify and check understanding and to find out how other cultures approach meetings.

9. Try to vary your intonation so that you sound interested.

10. Summarise often.

Use these checklists to help you prepare for an intercultural meeting.

PREPARATION CHECKLIST FOR INTERCULTURAL MEETINGS:
PROCEDURES

1.   What is the normal procedure for business meetings in that culture?

2.   Who will be at the meeting?

3.   Will the participants be able to make decisions themselves?

4.   Do they normally expect a decision to be made at the end of a meeting?

5.   Do they expect a lot of detailed written information before the meeting?

6.   How much time do they like to spend on small talk and relationship building before the normal business?

7.   Do meetings always start on time?

8.   Do they keep to a set agenda?

9.   Do they allow interruptions, such as phone calls and messages?

PREPARATION CHECKLIST FOR INTERCULTURAL MEETINGS:
FORMALITIES

1. How formal are they likely to be?

2. Are formal clothes expected?

3. How should I address the other participants: by using family names, or first names?

4. Are titles important?

5. How should I present and receive business cards?

PREPARATION CHECKLIST FOR INTERCULTURAL MEETINGS:
BEHAVIOUR

1. Do people from the other culture like to preserve harmony and avoid conflict?

2. Do people from the other culture hide what they really feel?

3. Are there any great differences in the use of body language, eye contact and gesture between my culture and theirs?

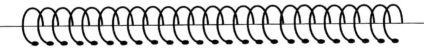

PREPARATION CHECKLIST FOR INTERCULTURAL MEETINGS:

COMMUNICATING AND SOCIALISING

1. Are there any potential problems in the use of language that I should be aware of?

2. Are there any sensitive subjects that I should avoid?

3. Will I be expected to socialise with the other participants after the formal meeting?

4. Are there any customs related to food and drink or present-giving that I should be aware of?

It is also useful to speak to people with experience of the relevant culture.

Formal meetings

8

Meetings can be either formal or informal. The procedure is different and there are special phrases in formal meetings. However, the language that we use for discussion is similar in both formal and informal meetings. The organiser of the meeting needs to consider:

- how to plan the formal meeting
- formal meetings procedure.

These are some of the differences between formal and informal meetings:

FORMAL	INFORMAL
Roles of participants: chair/chairperson recorder/note-taker, secretary	No formal roles, although someone will lead the meeting
Paperwork: formal invitations, agenda, working papers, minutes	Agenda, working papers, minutes
Time and place (venue) often arranged a long time in advance	Meetings often called at short notice
Length may be fixed	Length may not be fixed

 For examples of a formal invitation and an agenda, please see Chapter One: *Preparing for the meeting*

Planning a formal meeting

A meeting is usually planned by the chairperson and the secretary or by an adviser to the chairperson.

There are several matters to consider:

Giving notice of the meeting

Sometimes, a minimum number of days' notice must be given to all participants. For example, there may be a legal requirement to give at least twenty-one days' notice of a meeting of the shareholders of a company. This notice of a meeting will be sent to all shareholders if their addresses are known. Alternatively, the notice of the meeting might be advertised in a national newspaper.

Making sure there will be a quorum

A meeting might require a minimum number of participants in order to make decisions. This minimum number is a **quorum**. If a quorum is required, the minutes should record the fact that this number did attend. A suitable phrase to use is: **It was noted that a quorum was present.**

Deciding the agenda

The following items are on the agendas of most formal meetings:

- apologies for absence
- minutes of the previous meeting
- matters arising from the minutes
- any other business (AOB).

Someone unable to attend the meeting should inform the chairperson or the chairperson's assistant in advance. The first item on the agenda is usually when the chairperson tells the participants who the absentees are.

All participants should receive a copy of the minutes of the previous meeting with the new agenda. These are the official record of what was said and what was decided at the meeting. The participants should read the minutes to check that they are an accurate record of what happened at the meeting. If everyone agrees that the minutes are accurate, the chairperson signs a copy.

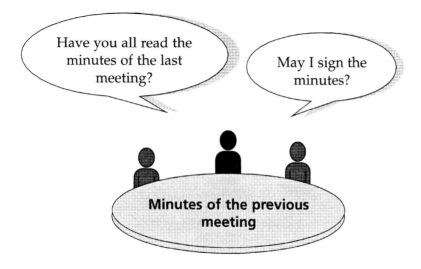

If someone thinks the minutes are inaccurate or incomplete, this is the time to say so.

I am not sure about item six. Is that really what happened?

I think there's a mistake on page three.

Decisions made and agreements reached at a meeting are recorded in the minutes. At the next meeting, the chairperson checks whether action has been taken to put these decisions and agreements into effect. In order to do this, s/he could say:

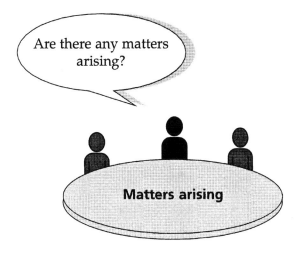

When the main items on the agenda have been discussed, the chairperson usually asks the other participants if there is anything else they would like to discuss before the meeting closes.

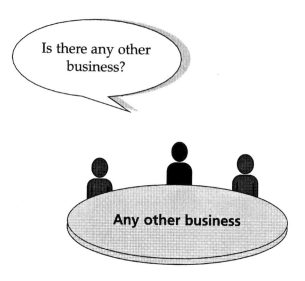

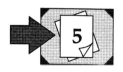 For other examples of a chairperson's duties and phrases to use, please see Chapter Five, *Chairing the meeting*

Formal meetings procedure

Formal meetings follow a set procedure and have certain rules which should be followed. The procedures and rules mentioned below are those commonly used in a British context, and sometimes in American meetings.

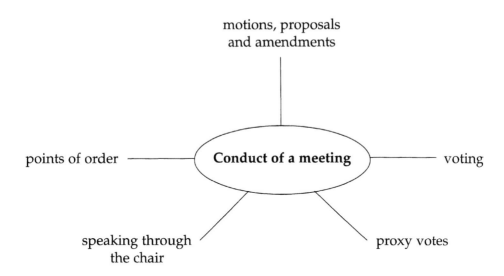

Motions, proposals and amendments

The participants at a meeting might be required to reach a decision about something. One way of reaching decisions is to put forward a **motion** or **proposal**.

One participant puts forward a motion and a second participant might be required to support the proposal (**second** the motion). **Amendments** may be made to proposals before a vote is taken.

Voting

A **vote** is then taken on the motion or proposal. Participants may vote **for** or **against** the proposal, or they may choose to **abstain** (not vote at all).

If there are more votes for the motion than votes against it, the motion is **carried** (accepted).

If there are more votes against the motion than for it, the motion is **rejected** (not accepted).

If a motion is rejected, another participant might put forward an **amendment**. This amendment will be put to a vote.

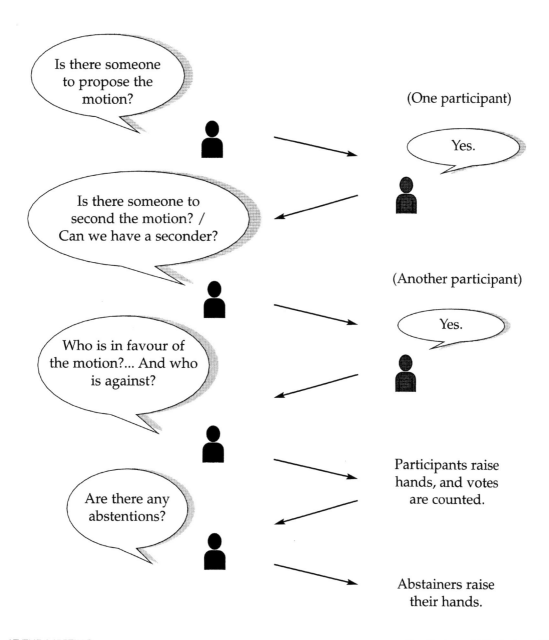

(One participant)

(Another participant)

Participants raise
hands, and votes
are counted.

Abstainers raise
their hands.

Proxy votes

A person entitled to vote may be unable to attend the meeting. Some formal meetings (for example, meetings of the shareholders of a company) allow these people to ask another person to vote at the meeting on their behalf. This is called **voting by proxy** or **proxy voting**. Proxy voting is only possible when the motions or proposals that will be put forward at the meeting are known in advance.

Speaking through the chair

At formal meetings, especially meetings with a large number of participants, the chairperson controls the conduct of a meeting. If someone wishes to say something when they have not been invited to do so, they may be required to attract the chairperson's attention for permission to speak.

This is known as **speaking through the chair**.

Points of order

A **point of order** is an interruption to the meeting when someone wishes to indicate that a formal rule has been broken or to correct something another participant has said but which may be factually incorrect. In order to do this, the participant may say:

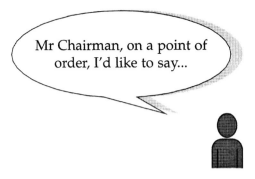

After the Meeting

SOUTHALL AND WEST
LONDON COLLEGE
LEARNING CENTRE

Following up the meeting

9

After the meeting, it is necessary to take follow-up action.

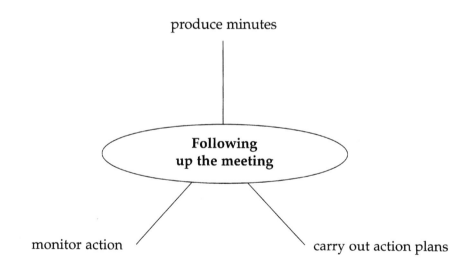

produce minutes

Following up the meeting

monitor action

carry out action plans

Producing minutes

Some communication after the meeting may be written and some may be verbal. Minutes are a written record of what has occurred at the meeting and the decisions that have been reached. Minutes remind participants of what has been agreed and any action that needs to be taken.

Minutes should be written as soon as possible after a meeting. This is necessary because you will more easily remember the important points, and also because the participants need to be reminded of what they must do.

Minutes should be accurate, objective, and clear.

The minutes may be a summary of the main points as in the example on the next page, or may be a much longer, more detailed document.

Although the style may be formal and the passive is sometimes used, in order to be concise, note form may be used.

Here is an example of the minutes of a meeting:

MINUTES OF THE PROJECT
TEAM MEETING HELD AT 18 PRINCES
STREET ON TUESDAY, 8 JUNE XXXX

Present

TR Smith, RP Davis, S Connor
BA Evans, MC Cross

Apologies for absence

Apologies for absence **were received** from KT Brown and TA Fielding. ——— Passive forms are used!

Minutes of the meeting held on 15 April XXXX

The minutes of the meeting held on 15 April XXXX **were agreed**. ———

Matters arising

None

Software development

BA Evans reported that... software would be introduced in all departments by September, XXXX.

Financial report

S Connor presented a report on the costs of the project. These are likely to be higher than planned. After some discussion, it was agreed that TR Smith and S Connor should prepare a report for the Board of Directors, asking for approval to exceed the budget by $200,000.

Action points

TR Smith and S Connor **to prepare** report as above, by 20 June, XXXX. ——— Notice the style: a short form is used <u>not</u> "are going to prepare"!

Date of next meeting

The next meeting will be held at 18 Princes Street on Tuesday, 6 July, XXXX at 09.00.

Action plans

After a meeting, there will usually be **action points**. This means the action to be taken if decisions have been made at the meeting. Certain people will be responsible for carrying out the action by a given date.

There will often be an **action plan**, a document that:

- lists the action to be taken
- identifies the people to perform the action (often with their initials only)
- identifies the deadlines by which the action should be completed.

An action plan may be included in the minutes of the meeting, or may be a separate document. Here is an example of an action plan:

ACTION PLAN		
1. New computer system to be purchased for the sales office	HA	15 August
2. New marketing plan to be prepared within four weeks	GM	31 August
3. Training programme to be arranged for members of the sales team	CD	31 August

At the subsequent meeting, the chairperson checks whether the action has been carried out as agreed at the previous meeting.

Monitoring action

This is an on-going process to check that the necessary action is being taken after the meeting, that people are adhering to deadlines, and that they know what they should do next. There may be:

- follow-up meetings
- interim reports
- daily checks.

Reviewing and evaluating the meeting

10

There are two kinds of evaluation which follow a meeting. One is the evaluation of the meeting and how it went. The other is personal evaluation of your own performance.

Evaluation of the meeting

After the meeting, it is useful to consider the following points:

- Did you achieve the objectives set at the beginning of the meeting?
- Did everyone make a contribution?
- Did you keep to the agreed procedures?

Evaluation of your performance

Whether you were the chairperson or a participant, you should carry out a review of your performance at the meeting. This should happen as soon as possible afterwards so that you do not forget what happened.

In particular, you should ask these questions:

- Did the meeting achieve what I expected?
- How effective was my performance?

When thinking about your performance, you should consider your use of language as well as what you have achieved. If you were the chairperson, you should also evaluate your management of the meeting. You will find useful checklists to help you evaluate your performance, either as chairperson or as a participant, on the following pages.

Use this checklist after a meeting to evaluate your participation in the meeting.

EFFECTIVE PARTICIPATION
EVALUATION CHECKLIST

1. Did I prepare carefully and was I well-informed about the subject of the meeting?

2. Did I communicate effectively?

3. Did I choose my language carefully?

4. Did I listen actively?

5. Did I show that I was listening?

6. Did I observe the speakers' reactions carefully, both by listening to their words, and watching their non-verbal messages?

7. Did I notice their reactions to me and to the meeting content and did I respond appropriately?

8. Did I think carefully about when to interrupt? Did I let speakers finish their points before interrupting?

EFFECTIVE PARTICIPATION
EVALUATION CHECKLIST

9. Did I talk too little / too much?

10. Was I argumentative or emotional?

11. Did I manage to separate the people from the problems?

12. Did I check that I had understood correctly before I agreed or disagreed with anyone?

13. Did I ask for clarification if I did not understand?

14. Did I make my points clearly and in simple language?

15. Did I remain positive?

16. Did I try to build bridges when there was a negative reaction?

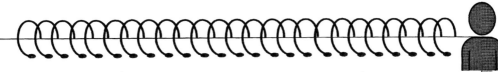

EFFECTIVE PARTICIPATION

EVALUATION CHECKLIST

17. Did I maintain eye contact with the other participants when I was speaking?

18. Did I look at other people when they were speaking?

19. Did I disagree diplomatically?

20. Did I ask for short breaks if I needed time to think about something?

21. Did I concentrate all the time or did I 'switch off' occasionally?

22. Am I satisfied with the results of the meeting?

23. If I attended the same meeting again, what would I do differently?

Use this checklist to evaluate your performance as chairperson.

EFFECTIVE CHAIRING OF A MEETING

EVALUATION CHECKLIST

1. Did I establish a good atmosphere by welcoming the participants and making sure they knew each other?

2. Did I clearly state the aims of the meeting?

3. Did I set the ground rules for the meeting?

4. Did I deal efficiently with the official procedures (if appropriate)? (e.g. apologies, previous minutes, matters arising, etc.)

5. Did I control the discussion well? (e.g. deal with interruptions, involve everyone)

6. Did I ensure that the agenda was adhered to?

7. Did I clarify points and check understanding?

EFFECTIVE CHAIRING OF A MEETING
EVALUATION CHECKLIST

8. Did I deal with voting procedures well (if appropriate)?

9. Did I check that everyone had reached agreement?

10. Did I summarise adequately?

11. Did I ensure that everyone was aware of the necessary action to take?

12. Did I check whether there was any other business?

13. Did I set the date of the next meeting?

14. Did I conclude the meeting positively and thank participants for their contributions?

15. If I chair another meeting, what will I do differently?